T0005679

THE FOSSIL WHISPERER

For my father, Aaron Becker. May his memory be a blessing. — H.B.
For Cedar and Frankie. I hope you always find treasures. — S.D.

Acknowledgments

A special thank-you to Wendy Sloboda, who so graciously answered all my interview questions during the research and writing of this book.

Text © 2022 Helaine Becker
Illustrations © 2022 Sandra Dumais

All rights reserved. No part of this publication may be reproduced, stored in a retrieval system or transmitted, in any form or by any means, without the prior written permission of Kids Can Press Ltd. or, in case of photocopying or other reprographic copying, a license from The Canadian Copyright Licensing Agency (Access Copyright). For an Access Copyright license, visit www.accesscopyright.ca or call toll free to 1-800-893-5777.

Pages 24–25: illustration based on a ROM photograph of *Wendiceratops pinhornensis* on display at the Royal Ontario Museum.

Published in Canada and the U.S. by Kids Can Press Ltd.
25 Dockside Drive, Toronto, ON M5A 0B5

Kids Can Press is a Corus Entertainment Inc. company

www.kidscanpress.com

The artwork in this book was rendered digitally.
The text is set in Picadilly.

Edited by Katie Scott
Designed by Marie Bartholomew

Printed and bound in Buji, Shenzhen, China, in 10/2021 by WKT Company

CM 22 0 9 8 7 6 5 4 3 2 1

FSC
www.fsc.org
MIX
Paper from
responsible sources
FSC® C010256

Library and Archives Canada Cataloguing in Publication

Title: The fossil whisperer : how Wendy Sloboda discovered a dinosaur / written by Helaine Becker ; illustrated by Sandra Dumais.

Names: Becker, Helaine, author. | Dumais, Sandra, 1977– illustrator.

Identifiers: Canadiana 20210203463 | ISBN 9781525304187 (hardcover)

Subjects: LCSH: Sloboda, Wendy — Juvenile literature. | LCSH: Ceratopsidae — Alberta — Juvenile literature. | LCSH: Dinosaurs — Alberta — Juvenile literature.

Classification: LCC QE862.O65 B43 2022 | DDC j567.915 — dc23

Kids Can Press gratefully acknowledges that the land on which our office is located is the traditional territory of many nations, including the Mississaugas of the Credit, the Anishnabeg, the Chippewa, the Haudenosaunee and the Wendat peoples, and is now home to many diverse First Nations, Inuit and Métis peoples.

We thank the Government of Ontario, through Ontario Creates; the Ontario Arts Council; the Canada Council for the Arts; and the Government of Canada for supporting our publishing activity.

THE FOSSIL WHISPERER

How Wendy Sloboda Discovered a Dinosaur

HELAINE BECKER

SANDRA DUMAIS

Kids Can Press

BRRRING!

Wendy had a rare eye for the unusual.
She saw things other people didn't. As soon
as the school bell trilled, she was up and out!

Into the hills.

Through the gullies.

On the hunt.

What was she hunting for?
Anything. Everything!

Gnarly rocks.

Buds and burrs.

The brilliant blue of a jay's feather.

Sometimes, Wendy took pictures of her discoveries with her new camera. Sometimes, she brought them home. She kept her favorite pictures on a shelf in her bedroom where she could always see them.

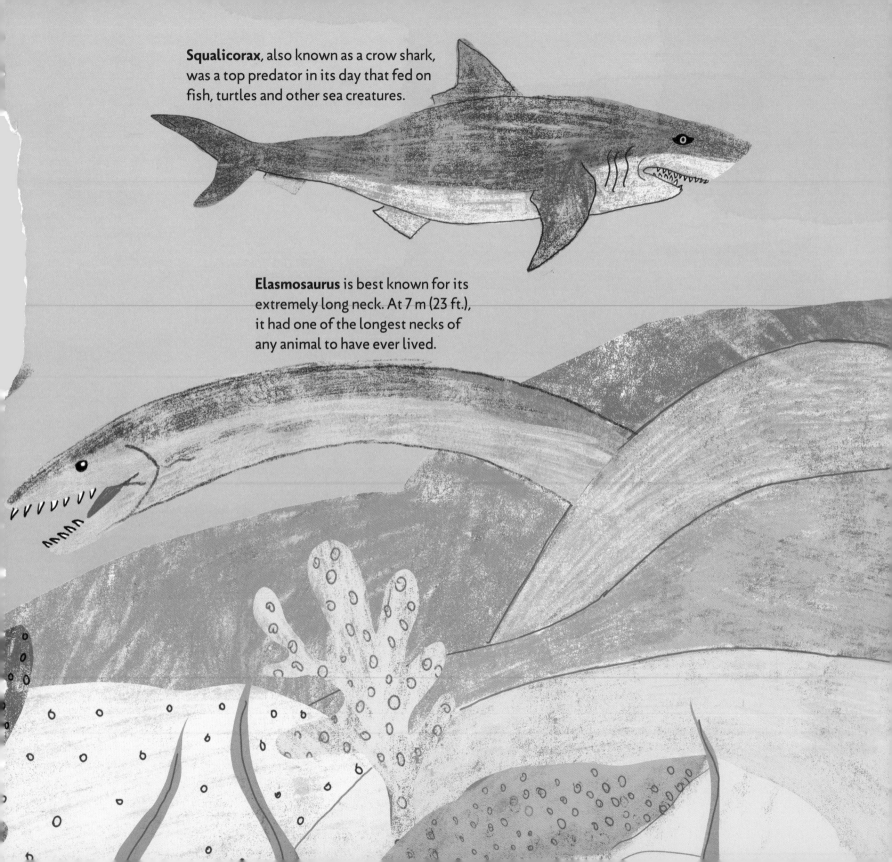

Squalicorax, also known as a crow shark, was a top predator in its day that fed on fish, turtles and other sea creatures.

Elasmosaurus is best known for its extremely long neck. At 7 m (23 ft.), it had one of the longest necks of any animal to have ever lived.

Archelon was a giant sea turtle that grew up to 3.7 m (12 ft.) long — twice the length of the largest sea turtle living today.

When Wendy was twelve, she went on a field trip to the badlands near her hometown in Alberta. Its hauntingly beautiful hoodoos were scoured by wind and time. And its deep coulees held fossils just waiting to be discovered.

Wendy spotted something unusual poking out of the ground. She brushed away the dirt and pried the object from its resting place.

"You have quite an eye," her teacher told her. "That's a piece of fossilized coral. Millions of years ago, this land was the Western Interior Seaway — an underwater world teeming with marine life."

Wendy was surprised and thrilled! What other fascinating stories could her discoveries tell?

Pachyrhizodus was a large tuna-like fish that was a ferocious predator with two rows of teeth for chomping on its prey.

From then on, Wendy spent more time among the windswept hoodoos, hunting for fossils. She loved exploring Devil's Coulee, a rugged ravine cut deep into the badlands.

Wherever she looked, Wendy saw what other people missed, such as a piece of bone that glimmered in the sun. She got better at distinguishing between the ordinary and the extraordinary and found more and more fossils — all that were left of the utterly strange creatures that had once roamed the earth.

One day, when Wendy was seventeen, she spotted something strange sticking out of the chalky ground. She knew it was special ... but what *was* it?

Wendy decided to ask her former teacher, who was now a university professor.

"You really do have quite an eye!" he told her.

Her find was rare: a fossilized dinosaur eggshell!

Paleontologists swarmed to Devil's Coulee, eager to find more fossils at the site. With big arm-juddering jackhammers and tiny delicate brushes, they uncovered fossilized eggs from a dinosaur called *Hypacrosaurus*.

Wendy wanted to learn more about how fossils revealed secrets from the past. She studied how to conserve them and decided to turn it into a career.

She got a job at the Royal Tyrrell Museum of Palaeontology and traveled the world, from Argentina to Greenland to Mongolia. Wendy became known as the "fossil whisperer" because she had a seemingly magical talent for discovering fossils wherever she went.

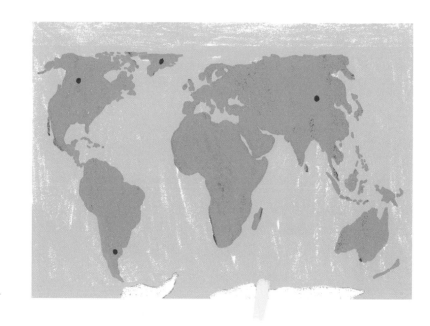

Daily Times

LEGENDARY FOSSIL WHISPE

THE POST
Wendy Sloboda!

WORLD NEWS
BREAKING NEWS!
Fossil Whisperer Discovers Ancient Turtle!!

Wendy Sloboda

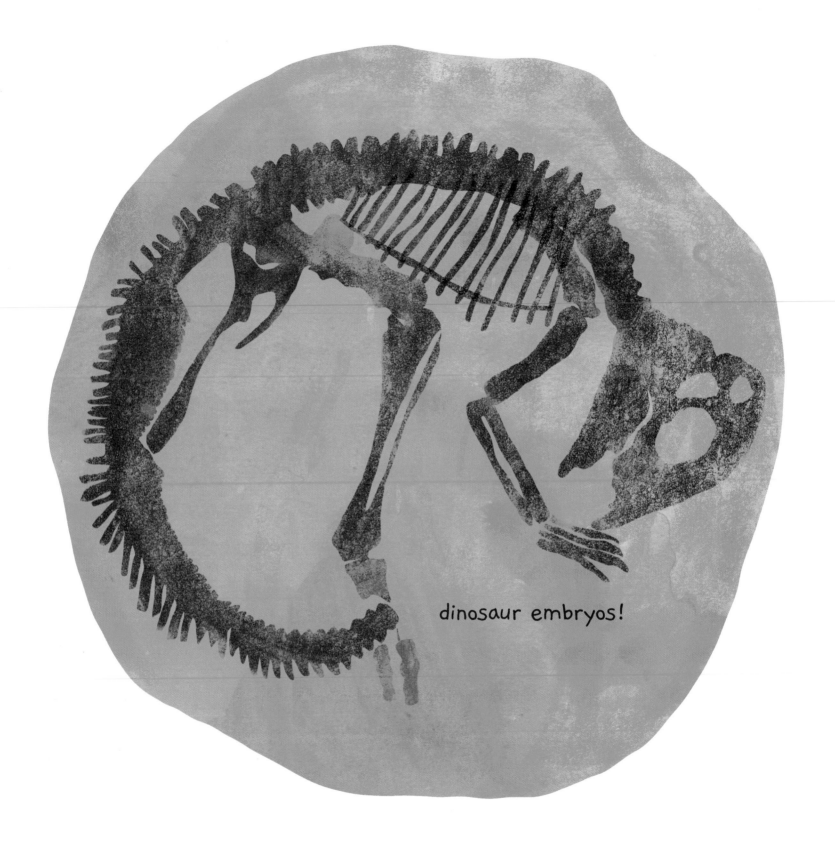

dinosaur embryos!

No one had ever seen *Hypacrosaurus* embryos in such superb condition. The discovery told a fascinating story about how these dinosaurs changed as they grew.
And it was all because of Wendy!

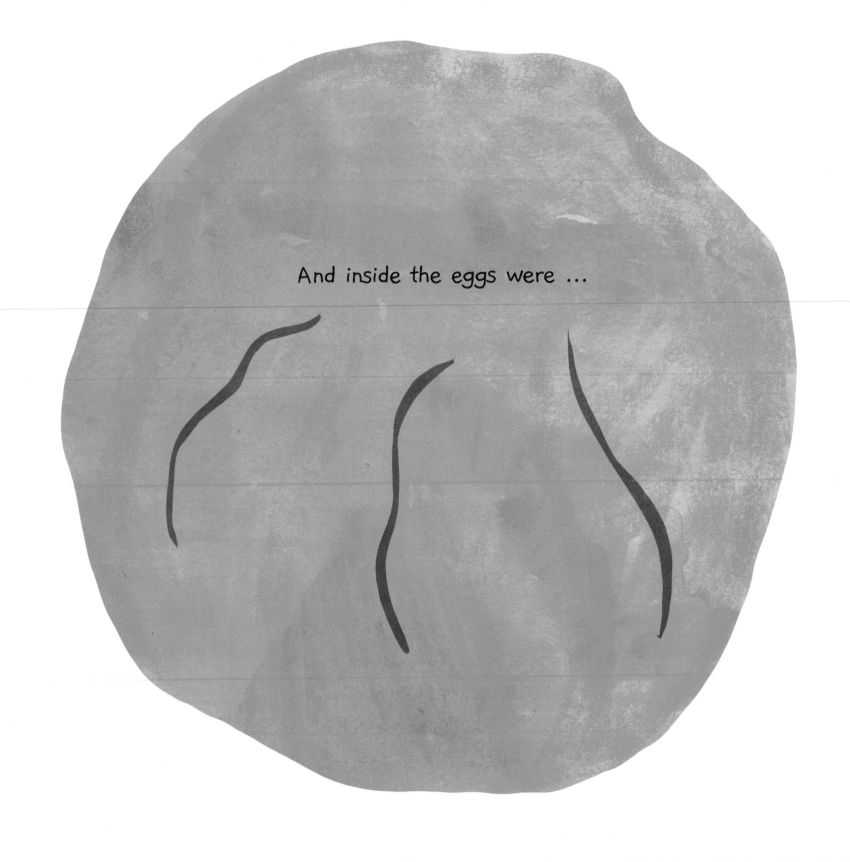

No matter how far she traveled, what Wendy loved most was searching for fossils near home. One day, while hunting near Alberta's Milk River, she spotted an unfamiliar shape glinting in the sunlight.

It was a skull fossil with a distinctive rough texture. She knew it came from a kind of horned dinosaur, like triceratops. But it was from a time long before triceratops had lived.

Excited, Wendy searched for more bones. She found them, buried deep in the rock. She would need help — and lots of it — to get them out.

It took more than four years for the excavation crew to remove all the bones from the hillside.

At last, scientists could begin to piece them together. When they did, they realized the bones were from an entirely new species of dinosaur, one no one had ever seen before!

The discovery exposed even more secrets from the past about how horned dinosaurs like this one had evolved.

WENDICERATOPS
LATE CRETACEOUS
*approx. 79 million
years ago*

This newly discovered dinosaur was so extraordinary, it needed an equally extraordinary name. The scientists agreed. It had to be named after Wendy.

Wendy found her own way to celebrate her discovery. And before long, she was up and out again!

Into the hills.

Through the gullies.

On the hunt.

She kept whispering to the fossils, searching for what secrets they would reveal next.

Wendiceratops pinhornensis

About the Real Wendy

Wendy Sloboda is widely recognized as one of the world's preeminent fossil hunters living today. Her finds have shed light on dinosaur evolution, especially in hadrosaurs, pterosaurs and ceratopsians.

Born and raised in Warner, Alberta, she made her first fossil discovery at age twelve while on a field trip to the Canadian Badlands, near her hometown. She later attended the University of Lethbridge, learning the skills to become a paleontology technician (someone who conserves and reconstructs fossils). To this day, she has found her most important specimens in Alberta.

Hunting for fossils is challenging, even for a professional like Wendy. During daylong hikes, she frequently encounters scorching heat, pelting hail, tornadoes, rattlesnakes and scorpions. But that hasn't stopped her from discovering more than three thousand fossils.

Wendy still scours the prime fossil-hunting territory near her home whenever she can, and often with her children. You can find her working in the field every summer on official digs for the Royal Tyrrell Museum.

How to Be a Fossil Hunter

You, too, can hunt for fossils — there are so many yet to be discovered! Like Wendy, you might find a missing piece of the story of life on Earth. Here's how to get started:

1. Find a fossil hot spot. You can try hunting in your own backyard, but if you want to take it up a notch, visit a local national park known for its abundant fossils.

2. Collect your tools. While your most valuable tool is your eyes, it helps to have the right gear:

- fossil field guide
- notebook and pencil
- safety goggles
- rock pick hammer
- chisel
- brush
- magnifying glass
- camera
- tissue paper (to wrap your fossil!)

3. Protect yourself from the elements. Depending on the weather, you may need protective clothing (hat, rain jacket, hiking shoes), sunscreen and bug spray. Pack a first aid kit for any scrapes, burns or bites.

4. Bring a buddy. Always go fossil hunting with another person, and make sure that someone at home knows where you are and how long you'll be gone.

5. Research the rules. In some places, it's illegal to remove fossils from where you find them. That's to help scientists preserve valuable information about where the fossils are found and to protect the land for environmental and cultural reasons. Know and follow the rules to help protect and preserve the land, its wildlife and its people.

Wendy's Key Fossil Discoveries

1982 (age 12)
Ancient coral
100 million years ago

1987
Hypacrosaurus eggshell
70 million years ago

1990
Hadrosaur skeleton
65 million years ago

1992
Pterosaur leg
77 million years ago

1999
Ancient turtles pregnant with eggs
75 million years ago

2002
Ankylosaur skull
70 million years ago

2003
Corythosaurus skull
76 million years ago

2003
Barrosopus slobodai[*] footprint
85 million years ago

2010
Wendiceratops skeleton
79 million years ago

2018
Albertochampsa skull
75 million years ago

[*]"Sloboda's muddy foot" — another species named after Wendy

Alberta's Amazing Bone Beds

Southern Alberta is a world-renowned hotbed of fossil discovery. It was once covered by the ocean. Later, it became a warm, lush landscape teeming with life. Thousands of plant and animal species thrived there for millions of years. Many have since gone extinct, including dinosaurs such as *Tyrannosaurus*, *Albertosaurus* and *Wendiceratops*. Their remains lie deep in the earth, buried beneath layers of sediment.

Today, southern Alberta is a rugged desert landscape scoured by wind. Extreme heat and cold crack and break up the stony ground. As rocks erode, long-buried fossils come up to the surface. The wind eats away the softer stone surrounding them and blows away the dust. After millions of years in hiding, these fossils can be discovered by scientists and curious people of all types — if, like Wendy, they have a keen eye.

How Are Fossils Formed?

Sometimes after an animal dies, its bones get buried under layers of soft sediment. Eventually, extreme pressure squeezes the sediment together until it becomes hard stone. Over time, the bones trapped within the stone dissolve, leaving an empty mold behind. When the mold gets filled with minerals, a fossil — a record in stone — is created.

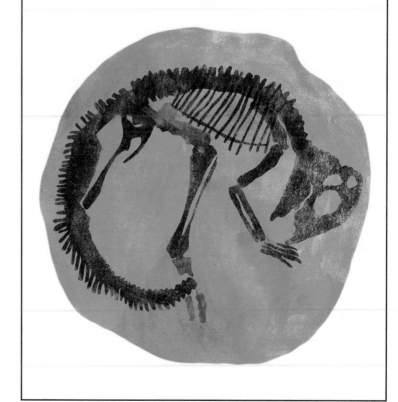

About *Wendiceratops*

Wendiceratops (Wendiceratops pinhornensis) lived in the area that's now southern Alberta about 79 million years ago, during the Late Cretaceous era. It measured 6 m (20 ft.) long and weighed about 1000 kg (2200 lb.).

Wendiceratops belonged to the same dinosaur family as triceratops: the ceratopsians. These herbivores lived mostly in herds and foraged for lush greenery along the seashore. They had a large, bony frill on their heads and a parrot-like beak. Many also had horns. But *Wendiceratops* is the oldest known dinosaur ever found to have a tall horn on its nose.

This distinctive horn helped paleontologists understand a missing link in the story of how ceratopsians evolved. Triceratops also had a large nose horn, but it lived about 10 million years later. Even more important, triceratops descended from a different branch of the ceratopsian family than *Wendiceratops*. That means large nose horns evolved at least *twice* in history, telling scientists that this distinct feature was even more important to survival than previously thought. Horns were probably used to fend off predators and in crucial battles between rivals for mates.

Today, you can see a reconstruction of the *Wendiceratops* skeleton, along with some of the original fossils, at the Royal Ontario Museum in Toronto, Canada.

With permission of the Royal Ontario Museum @ ROM.

Glossary

badlands: a type of dry terrain that is heavily eroded, with little vegetation

bone bed: layers of rock that contain a huge number of fossils

ceratopsians: a family of dinosaurs distinguished by a bony frill on the head and a nose horn

coulee: a ravine

embryo: an animal at the earliest stage of development, when it's still in the womb or egg

fossil: a stone cast made of an ancient plant or animal

hadrosaur: a duck-billed dinosaur that lived between 86 to 65 million years ago

herbivore: a plant-eating animal

hoodoo: a rock formation, usually shaped like a rugged column

Hypacrosaurus: a duck-billed dinosaur that lived between 75 to 67 million years ago

pterosaur: a large flying reptile that lived between 228 to 66 million years ago, alongside the dinosaurs

sediment: small particles of soil or dust that settle to the bottom of a liquid

Wendiceratops: a ceratopsian that lived approximately 79 million years ago

To Discover More

Books
Buzzeo, Toni. *When Sue Found Sue: Sue Hendrickson Discovers Her T. Rex*. Illustrated by Diana Sudyka. New York: Abrams Books for Young Readers, 2019.

Skeers, Linda. *Dinosaur Lady: The Daring Discoveries of Mary Anning, the First Paleontologist*. Illustrated by Marta Àlvarez Miguéns. Naperville, IL: Sourcebooks Explore, 2020.

Websites
Devil's Coulee Dinosaur & Heritage Museum
www.devilscoulee.com

Royal Ontario Museum
www.rom.on.ca

Royal Tyrrell Museum
www.tyrrellmuseum.com